2018 Ultimate Vegan Instant Pot Cookbook

5 Ingredients or Less- Easy & Delicious Plant-Based Recipes (Save Money and Time for Smart People)

Steve Lee

© Copyright 2017 -Steve Lee- All Rights Reserved.

In no way is it legal to reproduce, duplicate, or transmit any part of this document by either electronic means or in printed format. Recording of this publication is strictly prohibited, and any storage of this material is not allowed unless with written permission from the publisher. All rights reserved.

The information provided herein is stated to be truthful and consistent, in that any liability, regarding inattention or otherwise, by any usage or abuse of any policies, processes, or directions contained within is the solitary and complete responsibility of the recipient reader. Under no circumstances will any legal liability or blame be held against the publisher for any reparation, damages, or monetary loss due to the information herein, either directly or indirectly.

Respective authors own all copyrights not held by the publisher.

Legal Notice:
This book is copyright protected. This is only for personal use. You cannot amend, distribute, sell, use, quote or paraphrase any part or the content within this book without the consent of the author or copyright owner. Legal action will be pursued if this is breached.

Disclaimer Notice:

Please note the information contained within this document is for educational and entertainment purposes only. Every attempt has been made to provide accurate, up-to-date and reliable, complete information. No warranties of any kind are expressed or implied. Readers acknowledge that the author is not engaging in the rendering of legal, financial, medical or professional advice.

By reading this document, the reader agrees that under no circumstances are we responsible for any losses, direct or indirect, which are incurred as a result of the use of information contained within this document, including, but not limited to, errors, omissions, or inaccuracies.

Table of Contents

INTRODUCTION 8
WHY PRESSURE COOK? 9
INSTANT POT BASICS 11

INSTANT POT: EQUIPMENT AND SET UP 11
FUNCTION AND BUTTON OVERVIEW................................. 13
THE DIFFERENCE BETWEEN INSTANT POT AND OTHER PRESSURE COOKERS 15
BEFORE COOKING IN YOUR INSTANT POT 15
INSTANT POT FAQ 17
COOKING TIMETABLE 18

VEGAN BASICS 20

HISTORY OF MODERN VEGANISM 20
HOW VEGANISM HELPS YOUR BODY? 21
FOODS AND INGREDIENTS TO AVOID 24

VEGAN INSTANT POT RECIPES 26

BREAKFAST RECIPES 26
Corn Pudding 26
Sweet Potato Toast 28
Strawberry Oatmeal 29
Chia and Coconut Pudding 30
Banana and Almond Butter Giant Pancake 31
Vanilla and Maple Toast.. 33
Pomegranate Porridge 34

Breakfast Biscuit 35
BEAN RECIPES 37
   Tex Mex Beans 37
   Hash with Black Beans 38
   Garbanzo and Tahini Hummus 39
   Bean Nachos 41
   Lemony Herbed Bean Dip 42
   Refried Jalapeno Beans 43
   Garbanzo Bean Mash 44
   Garlicky Green Beans 45
GRAINS RECIPES 47
   Instant Steel Cut Oats 47
   Garlicky Polenta 49
   Tomato & Spinach Couscous 50
   Shallot and Paprika Grits 51
   Fig Millet 52
   Sweet Berry Quinoa 53
   Oats and Apricots 54
   Turmeric Brown Rice 55
SOUPS AND STEWS 56
   Mixed Veggie Soup 56
   Squash and Potato Soup 58
   Plantain and Red Bean Stew 59
   Lentil Chili 60
   Orange, Sweet Potato & Chickpea Stew 61
   Pomodoro Soup 62
   Corn and Onion Chowder 63
   Leek, Broccoli, and Potato Soup 64
VEGETABLE RECIPES 65
   Instant Ratatouille 65

    Kale and Sweet Potatoes with Tofu 67
    Pureed Chili Carrots 68
    Sesame Bok Choy 69
    Lemon Artichokes 70
    Broccoli and Mushrooms 71
    Tomato and Tofu Bake 72
    Potato Mash 73
MAIN DISH RECIPES 74
    Vegan White Pizza 74
    Mini Vegan Shephard's Pie 76
    Mushroom Pasta 78
    Basil Risotto 79
    Vegan Cheese and Asparagus Pasta 80
    Carrot and Sweet Potato Medley 81
    Pesto Farfale 82
    Mexican Rice Casserole 83
BURGER AND PATTIES 84
    Cauliflower Patties 84
    Mixed Veggie Patties 86
    Potato and Scallion Patties 88
    Eggplant Burgers 89
    Beet and Chickpea Burger Patties 91
    Zucchini Burgers 92
    Red Bean Burger Patties 93
    Corn Patties 94
SAUCE RECIPES 96
    Chili Sauce 96
    White Sauce 98
    Lentil Marinara Sauce 99
    Applesauce 100

    Bean Bolognese Sauce 101
    Tomato and Basil Sauce 102
    Mixed Veggie Sauce 103
    Vanilla Caramel Sauce 104
SNACK AND APPETIZERS RECIPES 105
    Lime and Garlic Kale "Chips" 105
    Street Corn on the Cob 107
    Turmeric Sweet Potato Sticks 108
    Boiled Peanuts 109
    Mini Mac and Cheese 110
    Turnip Alfredo Dip 111
    Instant Potato Slices 112
    Candied Pecans 113
DESSERT RECIPES 114
    Almond and Chocolate Candy 114
    Banana Bread 116
    Stuffed Peaches 117
    Cherry Pie 118
    Blueberry Lemon Compote 120
    Apple Tart 121
    Simple Apple and Coconut Balls 123
    Chocolate Muffins 124

CONCLUSION 125

Introduction

Thank you for downloading "*2018 Ultimate Vegan Instant pot Cookbook: 5 Ingredients or less-Easy & Delicious Plant-Based Recipes*".

If you are tired of energy-draining cooking, I promise that you will find nothing overwhelming in this book. The recipes are simple and easy, and all of them are made with 5 or less ingredients. And if that doesn't seem relieving, then perhaps this will – there is very little stirring and whisking involved. You simply dump a couple of ingredients in the Instant Pot and you let this revolutionary appliance do its magic. Mouthwatering results are guaranteed.

Being a must-have cookbook for every vegan, this book offers 80 incredibly delicious and simple-to-make plant-based meals that your whole family will love. No matter what time of the day it is and no matter if you are craving a sweet or savory meal, this book has you covered and keeps your cravings in check.

Sounds like a deal you cannot miss? Jump to the first chapter and learn all about pressure cooking for vegans.

I dare you to try to pick a favorite recipe!

Why Pressure Cook?

Many people still get the chills when they hear the word "pressure cooker". If you are one of the many who are frightened of food explosions in your kitchen, then you will be relieved to know that that era of pressure cooking is long gone. Modern pressure cookers are nothing like those the housewives used in the 1950s. Now we have electric pressure cookers that offer us nothing but benefits. If you do not own one, you have no idea what you have been missing out.

Pressure Cooking Saves You Time

No one wants to spend hours in the kitchen. Thanks to the even flow of pressure, the meals are cooked 2/3 of the time faster than on the stove or in the oven. I guess they should rename these appliances in *fast pressure cookers* because cooking takes a whole different meaning with these appliances. Busy people will definitely appreciate owning one.

Pressure Cooking Saves You Money

The fact that the food in a pressure cooker is prepared two times faster is a clear indicator that your electric bill will also be reduced. But that is not the only way that you can save money if you switch to pressure cooking. Electric pressure cookers have the capability to turn even the cheap and not so pretty-looking foods into restaurant-grade dishes that your pocket will absolutely love.

Pressure Cooking is Healthier

Do you know how half of the food nutrients get lost during the process of cooking? Well, that does not happen in the pressure cooker. Because of the even pressure flow, the food in the pressure cooker is cooked evenly, without losing its essential minerals and vitamins. You don't have to worry about overcooking broccoli ever again.

Another thing that you need to keep in mind is that switching to pressure cooking means no more worrying about harmful substances on the food. The electric pressure cookers cook above the temperature of boiling water which means that all of the hazardous compounds get destroyed during the cooking process.

Pressure Cooking is Convenient

Like I said, forget about whisking and stirring because pressure cooking is an absolutely hassle-free way of preparing your meals. Simply combine all of the ingredients in your pressure cooker and voila! An elegant and incredibly delicious meal can be served on the table in a jiffy.

Instant Pot Basics

At the first glance, the Instant Pot seems like a rather confusing machine. Multiple buttons and functions, and not much explanation in the user's manual. If you have bought an Instant Pot just to find it hard to crack the puzzle of pressure cooking, don't worry. This chapter will teach you all there is to know about Instant cooking and will turn you into a pressure cooking master in no time.

Instant Pot: Equipment and Set Up

Keep in mind that there are quite a few different versions of Instant Pot on the market but regardless of which appliance you own, they all come with similar gems that are hiding inside the packaging box:

- A Steamer Rack
- A Rice Paddle
- A Soup Scoop
- A Rice Measuring Cup
- A Condensation Collector
- A Quick Reference Guide
- A Recipe Book
- A User's Manual

After you unwrap the stainless steel insert, which is called the *inner pot*, you will have to wash it well along with the IP's *silicone ring*, *lid*, and all of the previously mentioned accessories.

<u>Important: The exterior of the Instant Pot can only be wiped clean. Do NOT immerse it in any liquid.</u>

Once all of the accessories have dried, it is time to set up the IP:

1. Insert the silicone ring in the lid's rack and make sure that it is sitting properly.
2. Check that all of the parts of the Instant Pot are functioning properly:
- The *Venting Knob* has to be attached and fully pushed down. Keep in mind that it is perfectly normal for the knob to be loose.
- The *Float Valve* should be easily popped down and up.
- The *Anti-Block Shield* should be easily pushed on the side and then lifted up.
3. Insert the steamer rack/trivet in the pot.

4. Install the condensation collecting plastic cup. There is a slot at the back of the IP where you should slide in the condensation collector.
5. Plug in the power cord of the IP.

Function and Button Overview

There are quite a few buttons on the Instant Pot but there are not there to make the cooking process overwhelming, but hassle-free. Each of these buttons has a default setting that can ease your pressure cooking even more:

<u>Manual Button</u> – The most used button of the IP, the manual button helps you set up the cooking time and pressure, manually.

<u>'+' and '-' Buttons</u> – With the help of these buttons, you can increase or decrease the time of cooking.

<u>Adjust Button</u> – The IP comes with some inbuilt default settings. This button helps you retrieve them all.

<u>Pressure Button</u> – You can easily switch form low to high and high to low pressure with a single click of this button.

<u>Keep Warm/Cancel</u> – Cancel the cooking time or keep the meal warm until ready to be served.

<u>Slow Cook Button</u> – Use the IP as a slow cooker with a click of this button.

Steam Button – Perfect for steaming veggies, the default cooking time for 10 minutes will make your cooking a lot easier.

Yogurt Button – Make yogurt or pasteurize milk with this button.

Rice Button – Its automatic setting of low pressure cooks rice to perfection.

Meat/Stew Button – If you want to make a stew or cook meat, with the inbuilt setting of 35 minutes, this button will definitely help you out.

Bean/Chili – Great for beans and chilies, the cooking time of 30 minutes will make your cooking a lot easier.

Poultry Button – *The inbuilt* setting of 15 minutes cooking time helps you cook juicy poultry.

Soup Button – With just a simple click on this button you can make nourishing soups in 30 minutes.

Multigrain Button – This button cooks grains to perfection for 40 minutes.

Porridge Button – This button is a convenient way of making porridges.

The Difference between Instant Pot and Other Pressure Cookers

If you have bought an Instant Pot, you have definitely made the best choice. And I am not saying this only for the previously mentioned benefits of pressure cooking that you will receive. The Instant Pot is way more than a pressure cooker. The reason why the Instant Pot wears the crown among its fellow pressure cookers is because it is actually a 7-in-1 appliance:

1. It is a Pressure Cooker
2. It is a Saute Pan
3. It is a Rice Cooker
4. It is a Slow Cooker
5. It is a Yogurt Maker
6. It is a Steamer
7. It is a Warming Pot

Before Cooking in Your Instant Pot

I am sure that you are eager to give your Instant Pot a try and whip up some tasty meals for your family, but the only way you can do that is by knowing the rules of cooking in the Instant Pot. Okay, I have just made that up. There aren't exactly any rules; you can learn through trial and error, but if you want to save yourself some time and learn the safest and most delicious way to prepare food in the IP, then you will definitely remember this:

Do NOT Overfill the Instant Pot

You may be tempted to increase the volume of the food you are about to cook in the IP, however, know that crowding the pot is actually a bad idea. Overfilling the Instant Pot can result in valve clogging and seriously increase the cooking pressure. Make sure never to fill it more than 2/3 of the way. And if you are making something that may increase its volume during cooking, then fill it only halfway through.

Do NOT Force Open the Lid

Electric pressure cookers are generally very safe, if you know how to use them, that is. Never force opens the lid. The pressure must be fully released before you open the lid; otherwise the hot steam may burn your hand.

The safest way to open the lid is by slowly tilting it away from you.

Do NOT Use Much Liquid

The Instant Pot needs liquid to cook under pressure, however, keep in mind that that liquid doesn't come from water only. For instance, if you decide to throw some tomatoes in the pot, you will need less liquid than if you cook the same meal without the tomatoes.

Using more liquid than necessary can only dilute the flavor and result in tasteless meals. Do not use more than 1 ½ cups of water when cooking dry ingredients, unless the recipes call otherwise.

Instant Pot FAQ

Here are the answers to some of the most frequent asked questions about the Instant Pot (that we haven't covered before). Hopefully, this will make Instant cooking an easier process for you.

Do I need to replace the sealing ring?

Yes. You should make a habit to check the rings before cooking, as they can deform after some time. It is recommended to replace them after 18 months.

Can I cook frozen foods in the Instant Pot?

Instant pot is great for cooking frozen food, especially since it allows you to skip the thawing process. Cook frozen foods like you normally cook, just keep in mind that you will need to increase the cooking time by a few minutes.

Why can I hear a clicking sound while cooking in the IP?

The clicking sound can happen due to one of these reasons:

- The power is switching on and off during the cooking process.
- Foods (such as dry beans) are popping open during the process of cooking.
- Possible frictions between the lid and the housing.
- Or it can be simply due to the moisture at the bottom of the inner pot.

Can I burn food in the Instant Pot?

Not likely. The IP comes with a burn-protection mechanism that works very successfully, except if the food is extremely high in starch content. The only way you can burn food is by leaving the food to cook on SAUTE unattended (just like you can burn the food on the stove).

Why does the release handle leak steam?

This is totally normal and safe. Because the contact between the pipe and the steam release handle is not fully sealed, it can happen for the handle to leak steam.

Should the steam release handle be so loose?

Yes. In order for it to function properly, the handle needs to be loose.

Cooking Timetable

Looking for a cheat sheet cooking timetable to make your life easier? These are the Instant Pot cooking times. You are welcome!

Food Type	Ready In
Beef Roast	35-40 minutes
Boneless Ribs	25 minutes
Pork Roast	45-55 minutes
Pork Chops	5 minutes
Whole Chicken	6 minutes per pound
Chicken Breasts	8 minutes
Chicken Thighs	9 minutes
Fish Fillets	2-3 minutes fresh, 3-4 minutes frozen
Dry Beans	26 minutes

Hard-Boiled Eggs	4 minutes
Quick Oats	5 minutes
Steel-Cut Oats	10 minutes
Pasta	4-5 minutes
Brown Rice	25 minutes
White Rice	12 minutes
Corn on the Cob	3-4 minutes
Whole Potatoes	12-15 minutes
Chopped Veggies	1-3 minutes

Vegan Basics

Whether you have just embarked the Veganism train or you have been a vegan your entire life, remembering the Vegan basics and its modern history can only be beneficial. If you are just starting your Vegan journey however, I strongly suggest you pay a good attention to this chapter and see why deciding to go all plant-based is definitely the right choice.

History of Modern Veganism

The World Vegan Day is on November the 1st, and each year there are more and more people who celebrate this animal-free movement. But what exactly does being a vegan mean and when did this movement exactly begin?

We all know what vegetarianism is. Not eating meat. Think of veganism as an extreme form of vegetarianism where besides meat, no other food or clothing that comes from animals or even includes an animal is used.

Thanks to its rapid growth in popularity, people believe veganism to be a new and modern movement, however, the roots of this diet can be traced back to the ancient civilizations. But even though ancient Buddhist advocated that people should not do harm to animals, despite for health reasons, veganism were not a thing until the middle of the 20th century.

That doesn't mean that everyone ate eggs and drank milk, but that since the term 'vegetarians' was formed in the 1847, almost 100 years vegans and vegetarians were dumped in the same category. Until Donald Watson, a British woodworker became tired of the confusions and decided to invent a new term for those people that didn't consume dairy and eggs – *vegans*.

A couple of years after the invention of the term *veganism*, the diet received a formal definition and explanation, which is when modern veganism started.

Like I said, veganism is really a rapidly-growing movement – with just a few millions followers in the early 1990s, the veganism community increased to incredible 550-950 million worldwide vegans in 2016 (according to Wikipedia). Over the last 5 years alone, the number of Vegans in the United Kingdom has increased over 300 percent, which is quite astonishing.

How Veganism Helps Your Body?

It seems that it is really growing rapidly in popularity. But is Vegan just a new craze and a trend that it is popular to follow? Or is being a vegan really beneficial and worth the sacrifice (for those who love meat)? What makes veganism so appealing?

First of all, if you are starting your Veganism journey just because you think it's cool, you are destined to fail. In order for you to be a real Vegan, you need to know what you are getting yourself into. And no, I am not talking about the life without animal products, but about the benefits that this diet can bring.

So, to keep it shorts – *yes*. Veganism is truly beneficial. Here are some of the most important ways in which being a vegan can being a vegan can bring true benefits to your body and overall health:

Zero Animal Fats

Diabetes, cholesterol, high blood pressure, cancers, heart disease, arthritis... Should I really go on? Animal fat has been linked to many, many health conditions and illnesses. Cutting back on animal products seriously reduces your risks of these illneses.

Bone Health

Despite the myth that vegans do not get enough calcium since they do not consume dairy products, the truth is actually quite the opposite. Vegans are actually more efficient at absorbing calcium and other nutrients in charge for the bone health, just because they do not consume animal products.

Calcium can be found in numerous plant-based products that are even better at providing you with the essential nutrients as dairy. Such foods are: kale, figs, spinach, black-eyed peas, turnip greens, soy milk, almond milk, etc.

Heart Health

Vegans are known to consume fewer calories. Thanks to the fact that they have leaner bodies and lower BMI (body mass index), their risk of obesity and other similar conditions is seriously reduced which contributes to balanced heart health.

Despite these benefits, being a vegan can also bring reduced risks of:

- Breast Cancer
- Colon Cancer
- Prostate Cancer
- Cholesterol
- Diabetes
- Arthritis
- Osteoporosis
- Macular Degeneration
- Cataracts

Veganism also provides a number of physical health benefits:

- Leaner body
- Expanded lifespan
- More energy
- Healthy skin
- Stronger hair and nails
- Alleviation of allergy symptoms

- Less intense PMS symptoms
- Reduced body odor and bad breath

Foods and Ingredients to Avoid

Veganism means staying away from any product that is made of animals or that includes animals in any way. If you are new to veganism this may be a bit confusing. For that purpose, I have created this list of foods and other ingredients that every vegan should avoid:

- Meat (red meat, poultry, processed meat)
- Fish and Shellfish
- All Dairy Products (milk, cheese, yogurt, butter, cream, ice cream, etc.)
- Eggs
- Bee products (honey, royal jelly, bee polen, etc.)
- Regular Mayonnaise
- Gelatine
- Natural flavoring (many of these ingredients are animal-based)
- Certain additives (such as E120, E322, E542, E904, E422, E631, E471, E901, etc.)
- Omega-3 fatty Acids (most of these fats come from fish, so be careful)

- Vitamin D3 (this vitamin is mostly derived from fish oil or the sheep's wool. The vegan alternative is derived from lichen)
- Dairy Ingredients (lactose, whey, and casein are all derived from dairy)
- Shellac (the shellac is secreted by the lac insect. It is mostly used to make food glaze or wax coating).
- Isinglass (this is a gelatin-like substance that is usually made from fish bladders)
- Cochineal and Carmine (The red color in most food products is actually made from the carmine that is made from ground cochineal insects)

Other products that may contain animal ingredients, but not always do are:

- Pesto sauce
- Bread products
- French Fries
- Some Sweets and candy
- Beer and wine
- Worcestershire sauce
- Roasted peanuts
- Deep-fried food

Vegan Instant Pot Recipes

Breakfast Recipes

Corn Pudding
(Total Time: 35 MIN | Serves: 2)

Ingredients:

- 1 cup Corn Kernels
- 3 tbsp Cornmeal
- 1 cup Coconut Milk
- 2 Shallots, chopped
- 1 ½ cups Water

Directions:

1. Grease your Instant Pot with some cooking spray and set it to SAUTE.
2. Add the shallots and cook until they become soft.
3. Stir in the corn kernels, coconut milk, and cornmeal.
4. Transfer the mixture to a baking dish and cover with a piece of aluminum foil.
5. Pour the water into the IP and lower the trivet.
6. Place the covered dish on the trivet and close the lid.

7. Cook the corn pudding on MANUAL for about 25 minutes.
8. Do a quick pressure release.
9. Serve and enjoy!

(Calories 170 | Total Fats 4.4g | Carbs 28.6 g | Protein 4.4g | Fiber: 2.8g)

Sweet Potato Toast

(Total Time: 30 MIN | Serves: 4)

Ingredients:

- 2 Sweet Potatoes, cut into slices
- 3 tbsp Vegan Butter
- 1 tsp Turmeric Powder

Directions:

1. Peel and slice the sweet potatoes.
2. Set your Instant Pot to SAUTE and melt 1 tbsp of the butter in it.
3. Add 1/3 of the sweet potato slices and saute until browned on all sides.
4. Transfer to a plate and repeat with the remaining ingredients.
5. Sprinkle the sweet potato toasts with turmeric powder and top with your favorite toppings (suggestion: diced veggies and coconut cream).
6. Serve and enjoy!

(Calories 140 | Total Fats 4 g | Carbs 32g | Protein 2.5g | Fiber: 5g)

Strawberry Oatmeal

(Total Time: 20 MIN | Serves: 4)

Ingredients:

- A handful of Strawberries chopped
- 2 cups Rolled Oats
- 4 cups Water
- 1 tbsp Maple Syrup
- 2 tbsp Flax Meal

Directions:

1. Place all of the ingredients in your Instant Pot.
2. Give it a good stir to combine well.
3. Close the lid and set the IP to MANUAL.
4. Cook on HIGH for 3 minutes.
5. Let the pressure drop on its own. This should take about 10 minutes.
6. Divide between 4 serving bowls.
7. Top with some sliced strawberries, if desired.
8. Enjoy!

(Calories 200 | Total Fats 3g | Carbs 31g | Protein 6g | Fiber: 6g)

Chia and Coconut Pudding

(Total Time: 45 MIN | Serves: 4)

Ingredients:

- ½ cup Chia Seeds
- ¼ cup Coconut Flakes
- 3 ½ tbsp chopped Almonds
- 4 tsp Sugar
- 2 cups Coconut Milk

Directions:

1. Dump everything in the instant pot.
2. Stir to combine the ingredients well.
3. Close the lid of the IP and set it to MANUAL.
4. Cook on HIGH for 3 minutes.
5. Release the pressure quickly.
6. Serve topped with favorite fruits.
7. Enjoy!

(Calories 130 | Total Fats 12g | Carbs 3g | Protein 14g | Fiber: 0.5g)

Banana and Almond Butter Giant Pancake

(Total Time: 45 MIN | Serves: 4)

Ingredients:

- 1 Banana, peeled
- ½ cup Creamy Almond Butter
- 1 cup Almond Milk
- ½ cup Buckwheat Flour

Directions:

1. Place all of the ingredients in a blender or a food processor.
2. Blend until the mixture becomes smooth.
3. Pour some water into the bottom of your Instant Pot (1-2 cups).
4. Grease a round baking dish that can fit into the IP with some cooking spray.
5. Pour the blended mixture into the dish.
6. Place the dish on the lowered trivet and close the lid.
7. Cook the giant pancake for about 40 minutes on LOW.
8. Release the pressure quickly.
9. Serve and enjoy!

(Calories 282 | Total Fats 18.6g | Carbs 26g | Protein 7.3g | Fiber: 6g)

Vanilla and Maple Toast

(Total Time: 10 MIN | Serves: 2)

Ingredients:

- 2 Bread Slices
- 1 tsp Vanilla Extract
- 2 tbsp Maple Syrup
- 2 tbsp Vegan Butter

Directions:

1. Combine the maple syrup and vanilla.
2. Brush the mixture over the bread slices making sure to coat all sides.
3. Melt the butter in the Instant Pot on SAUTE.
4. Add the bread slices and cook for about 2 minutes per side.
5. Top with your favorite toppings on serve on its own.
6. Enjoy!

(Calories 224 | Total Fats 0.8g | Carbs 26g | Protein 2.3g | Fiber: 0.7g)

Pomegranate Porridge

(Total Time: 10 MIN | Serves: 4)

Ingredients:

- 1 ½ cups Water
- 2 cups Oats
- 1 ½ cups Pomegranate Juice
- 2 tbsp Pomegranate Molasses

Directions:

1. Place all of the ingredients in your Instant Pot.
2. Stir to combine the mixture well.
3. Close the lid and set your Instant Pot to MANUAL.
4. Cook on HIGH for 3-4 minutes.
5. Release the pressure quickly.
6. Serve and enjoy!

(Calories 400 | Total Fats 6g | Carbs 70g | Protein 14g | Fiber: 6.3g)

Breakfast Biscuit

(Total Time: 45 MIN | Serves: 4)

Ingredients:

- 1 cup plus 2 tbsp Self-Rising Flour
- ½ cup Vegan Butter
- ¾ cup Vanilla Almond Milk
- 1 ½ cups Water
- 3 tbsp Coconut Sugar

Directions:

1. Pour the water into the Instant Pot and then lower the trivet.
2. Combine the sugar and flour in a bowl.
3. Add the butter and rub it with your fingers until a crumbly mixture is formed.
4. Gradually add the milk, kneading with your hand to incorporate everything well.
5. Roll out the dough on a flat, clean, and lightly floured surface.
6. Cut the biscuits with a cookie cutter or simply cut them in squares with a knife.
7. Line a baking dish that can fit into the IP, with some parchment paper.
8. Arrange the biscuits on the dish and place it on the lowered trivet.

9. Close the lid and set the IP to MANUAL.
10. Cook on HIGH for 10 minutes.
11. Serve and enjoy!

(Calories 200 | Total Fats 19g | Carbs 20g | Protein 5g | Fiber: 2g)

Bean Recipes

Tex Mex Beans

(Total Time: 35 MIN | Serves: 6)

Ingredients:

- 20 ounces Pinto Beans
- 1 Onion, diced
- 5 cups Veggie Broth
- 1 packet Taco Seasoning
- ½ cup Salsa Verde

Directions:

1. Place all of the ingredients in the Instant Pot.
2. Give the mixture a good stir to combine well.
3. Close the lid and set the IP to MANUAL.
4. Cook for 12 minutes on HIGH.
5. Let the pressure come down naturally, about 15 minutes.
6. Drain the excess cooking liquid before serving.
7. Enjoy!

(Calories 436 | Total Fats 6g | Carbs 66g | Protein 28g | Fiber: 9g)

Hash with Black Beans

(Total Time: 15 MIN | Serves: 4)

Ingredients:

- 2 cups grated Sweet Potatoes
- 1 cup canned Black Beans, drained
- ½ cup Veggie Broth
- 1 tbsp Olive Oil
- 1 Onion, diced

Directions:

1. Heat the oil in your Instant Pot on SAUTE.
2. Add the onions and cook for a few minutes, until they become soft.
3. Stir in the sweet potatoes, black beans, and veggie broth.
4. Close the lid and set the IP to MANUAL.
5. Cook the bean hash for 2-3 minutes on HIGH.
6. Release the pressure quickly.
7. Serve and enjoy!

(Calories 133 | Total Fats 9g | Carbs 28g | Protein 5g | Fiber: 4g)

Garbanzo and Tahini Hummus

(Total Time: 45 MIN | Serves: 4)

Ingredients:

- Juice from 1 Lemon
- 1 cup Garbanzo Beans, soaked overnight and rinsed
- 6 cups Water
- 3 Garlic Cloves, crushed
- 2 tbsp Tahini

Directions:

1. Combine the water, garlic, and garbanzo beans, in the Instant Pot.
2. Close the lid and set the IP to MANUAL.
3. Cook the beans for 18 minutes on HIGH.
4. Let the pressure drop naturally.
5. Place the drained bean in a food processor, but reserve the cooking liquid.
6. Add half of the liquid to the food processor, along with the lemon juice and tahini.
7. Pulse and keep adding some of the liquid, until the hummus reach the consistency that you desire.
8. Serve and enjoy!

(Calories 109 | Total Fats 4g | Carbs 15g | Protein 13g | Fiber: 4g)

Bean Nachos

(Total Time: 35 MIN | Serves: 6)

Ingredients:

- 2 cups Pinto Beans
- 3 cups Veggie Broth
- 1 Onion, quartered
- 1 tsp Cumin
- ½ cup Cilantro Salsa

Directions:

1. Combine all of the ingredients in your Instant Pot.
2. Set the IP to MNAUAL.
3. Cook the beans on HIGH for 25 minutes.
4. Do a natural pressure release, for about 10 minutes.
5. Transfer the mixture to a food processor and pulse until smooth.
6. Serve as desired and enjoy!

(Calories 263 | Total Fats 11g | Carbs 45g | Protein 17g | Fiber: 6g)

Lemony Herbed Bean Dip

(Total Time: 25 MIN | Serves: 4)

Ingredients:

- 1 ½ cups Great Northern Beans, soaked overnight and drained
- 1 tbsp Cumin
- 1/3 cup Lemon Juice
- ¼ cup minced Cilantro

Directions:

1. Place the drained beans in your Instant Pot.
2. Add enough water to cover them by 1 inch.
3. Close the lid and set your Instant Pot to MANUAL.
4. Cook the beans for 13 minutes on HIGH.
5. Let the pressure release naturally.
6. Drain the beans and place them in a food processor.
7. Add the lemon juice and cumin and pulse until smooth.
8. Stir in the minced cilantro.
9. Serve and enjoy!

(Calories 500 | Total Fats 23g | Carbs 50g | Protein 18g | Fiber: 5g)

Refried Jalapeno Beans

(Total Time: 45 MIN | Serves: 4)

Ingredients:

- 1 pound dry Beans (this recipe uses Pinto Beans), soaked for 30 minutes
- 2 cups Vegetable Broth
- 1 Jalapeno, seeded and diced
- ¾ cup diced Onion
- 1 tsp Cumin

Directions:

1. Drain the beans and place them in the Instant Pot.
2. Add the remaining ingredients and stir well to combine.
3. Close the lid and set your Instant Pot to BEAN/CHILI.
4. Cook the beans for 45 minutes.
5. Let the pressure come out naturally.
6. Blend the mixture with a hand blender (optional).
7. Serve and enjoy!

(Calories 230 | Total Fats 9g | Carbs 35g | Protein 12g | Fiber: 4g)

Garbanzo Bean Mash

(Total Time: 20 MIN | Serves: 3)

Ingredients:

- 1 ¾ cup Garbanzo Beans
- ¼ cup toasted Pumpkin Seeds
- ½ tbsp ground Mustard
- 2 Garlic Cloves, quartered

Directions:

1. Place the garbanzo beans in your Instant Pot.
2. Add enough water to cover them completely.
3. Close he lid and set the IP to BEAN/CHILI.
4. Cook the beans for 13 minutes.
5. Release the pressure quickly.
6. Drain the beans, but reserve some of the liquid.
7. Transfer the beans to a food processor.
8. Add the pumpkin seeds, garlic, mustard, and 2-3 tablespoons of the cooking liquid.
9. Pulse until smooth.
10. Serve and enjoy!

(Calories 180 | Total Fats 8g | Carbs 26g | Protein 4g | Fiber: 4g)

Garlicky Green Beans

(Total Time: 20 MIN | Serves: 4)

Ingredients:

- 1 cup Water
- 2 tbsp White Wine Vinegar
- 1 pound Green Beans
- 3 tsp minces Garlic
- 3 tbsp Olive Oil

Directions:

1. Pour the water into the Instant Pot.
2. Add the beans and close the lid.
3. Set the IP to MANUAL and cook the beans on HIGH for 2 minutes.
4. Release the pressure quickly.
5. Transfer the beans to a serving bowl and discard the cooking liquid.
6. Wipe the IP clean and add the olive oil.
7. Heat it on SAUTE.
8. Add the garlic and cook for 30-60 seconds.
9. Press CANCEL and stir in the vinegar.
10. Drizzle this mixture over the green beans.
11. Serve and enjoy!

(Calories 145 | Total Fats 11g | Carbs 9g | Protein 3.5g | Fiber: 2g)

Garlicky Green Beans

(Total Time: 20 MIN | Serves: 4)

Ingredients:

- 1 cup Water
- 2 tbsp White Wine Vinegar
- 1 pound Green Beans
- 3 tsp minces Garlic
- 3 tbsp Olive Oil

Directions:

1. Pour the water into the Instant Pot.
2. Add the beans and close the lid.
3. Set the IP to MANUAL and cook the beans on HIGH for 2 minutes.
4. Release the pressure quickly.
5. Transfer the beans to a serving bowl and discard the cooking liquid.
6. Wipe the IP clean and add the olive oil.
7. Heat it on SAUTE.
8. Add the garlic and cook for 30-60 seconds.
9. Press CANCEL and stir in the vinegar.
10. Drizzle this mixture over the green beans.
11. Serve and enjoy!

(Calories 145 | Total Fats 11g | Carbs 9g | Protein 3.5g | Fiber: 2g)

Grains Recipes

Instant Steel Cut Oats

(Total Time: 10 MIN | Serves: 4)

Ingredients:

- 1 cup Coconut Milk
- 1 cup Steel Cut Oats
- 3 cups Water
- 2 tsp Coconut Sugar
- Pinch of Sea Salt

Directions:

1. Pour 1 cup of the water into the Instant Pot.
2. In a baking dish or a heatproof bowl, combine the oats with the remaining water.
3. Place the bowl on the trivet, lower it, and close the lid.
4. Set the Instant Pot to MANUAL.
5. Cook the oats on HIGH for 6 minutes.
6. Do a quick pressure release.
7. Stir in the coconut milk, salt, and sugar.
8. Serve topped with your favorite toppings.
9. Enjoy!

(Calories 155 | Total Fats 2g | Carbs 28g | Protein 4g | Fiber: 5.3g)

Garlicky Polenta

(Total Time: 30 MIN | Serves: 4)

Ingredients:

- 2 cups Corn Meal
- 3 cups Hot Water
- 4 cups Veggie Stock
- 4 tsp minced Garlic
- 1 tsp Paprika

Directions:

1. Set your Instant Pot to SAUTE.
2. Add garlic, paprika, and just a splash of the hot water.
3. Cook for a minute until the mixture becomes fragrant.
4. Add the remaining ingredients.
5. Give it a good stir to combine.
6. Close the lid and set the IP to MANUAL.
7. Cook the polenta for 10 minutes.
8. Release the pressure naturally, about 10 minutes.
9. Serve and enjoy!

(Calories 200 | Total Fats 8g | Carbs 19g | Protein 14g | Fiber: 4g)

Tomato & Spinach Couscous

(Total Time: 15 MIN | Serves: 4)

Ingredients:

- 8 ounces Couscous
- 1 ¼ cup Vegetable Broth
- 1 ½ Tomato, chopped
- ½ cup chopped Spinach
- 2 tbsp Vegan Butter

Directions:

1. Melt the butter in the IP on SAUTE.
2. Add the couscous and cook for a minute.
3. Pour the broth over and stir to combine.
4. Close the lid and set the Instant Pot to MANUAL.
5. Cook for 5 minutes on HIGH.
6. Do a quick pressure release.
7. Transfer the couscous to a bowl.
8. Stir in the tomato and spinach.
9. Serve and enjoy!

(Calories 230 | Total Fats 3g | Carbs 36g | Protein 7.3g | Fiber: 5g)

Shallot and Paprika Grits

(Total Time: 30 MIN | Serves: 3)

Ingredients:

- 1 cup Quick Cooking Grits
- 2 Shallots, diced
- 1 ½ tsp Smoked Paprika
- 2 tbsp Coconut Oil
- 3 cups Vegetable Broth

Directions:

1. Melt the coconut oil in the Instant Pot on SAUTE.
2. Add the shallots and cook for 3 minutes.
3. Stir in paprika and saute for 30 seconds more.
4. Add the grits and cook for about 1 minute.
5. Pour the broth over and give it a good stir to combine.
6. Close the lid and set the IP to MANUAL.
7. Cook on HIGH for 6 minutes.
8. Do a quick pressure release.
9. Serve and enjoy!

(Calories 210 | Total Fats 8g | Carbs 21g | Protein 4g | Fiber: 3.5g)

Fig Millet

(Total Time: 20 MIN | Serves: 4)

Ingredients:

- 1 ¾ cups Millet
- 1/3 cup chopped dried Figs
- 1 cup Almond Milk
- 2 cups Water
- 2 tbsp Coconut Oil

Directions:

1. Combine all of the ingredients in your Instant Pot.
2. Close the lid and set your Instant Pot to SOUP.
3. Cook the millet for 10 minutes.
4. Let the pressure drop naturally.
5. Fluff the mixture with a fork and stir well before serving.
6. Enjoy!

(Calories 310 | Total Fats 10g | Carbs 33g | Protein 5g | Fiber: 5g)

Sweet Berry Quinoa

(Total Time: 35 MIN | Serves: 4)

Ingredients:

- 1 cup Raw Quinoa
- 4 cups Water
- 4 tbsp Maple Syrup
- ½ cup Berry Mix (this recipe used Blueberries and Strawberries)
- ½ tsp Vanilla Extract

Directions:

1. Combine the water and quinoa in the Instant Pot.
2. Close the lid and set your IP to PORRIDGE.
3. Cook on the default setting.
4. Release the pressure naturally. This should take about 10 minutes.
5. Fluff the quinoa with a fork.
6. Stir in the vanilla and maple.
7. Top with the berries.
8. Serve and enjoy!

(Calories 203 | Total Fats 7g | Carbs 45g | Protein 8g | Fiber: 6g)

Oats and Apricots

(Total Time: 10 MIN | Serves: 4)

Ingredients:

- 1 cup Rolled Oats
- 2 Apricots, diced
- 2 ½ cups Coconut Milk
- ¼ tsp Cinnamon

Directions:

1. Place all of the ingredients in your Instant Pot.
2. Stir to combine well and close the lid.
3. Set the Instant Pot to MANUAL.
4. Cook the oats on HIGH for 3 minutes.
5. Let the pressure come out naturally.
6. Serve and enjoy!

(Calories 240 | Total Fats 4g | Carbs 22g | Protein 4.5g | Fiber: 4.5g)

Turmeric Brown Rice

(Total Time: 30 MIN | Serves: 6)

Ingredients:

- 2 cups Brown Rice
- 2 tsp Turmeric Powder
- 3 cups Vegetable Stock
- 1 Carrot, diced
- 1 Shallot, diced

Directions:

1. Add some of the stock, carrot and shallot in your Instant Pot.
2. Set it to SAUTE and cook for a couple of minutes.
3. Stir in the rice, turmeric, and the remaining stock.
4. Close the lid and set the IP to MANUAL.
5. Cook the rice on LOW for 22 minutes.
6. Release the pressure quickly.
7. Fluff with a fork before serving.
8. Serve and enjoy!

(Calories 270| Total Fats 3g | Carbs 50g | Protein 7g | Fiber: 7g)

Soups and Stews

Mixed Veggie Soup
(Total Time: 25 MIN | Serves: 6)

Ingredients:

- 12 ounces Frozen Mixed Veggies (carrots, broccoli, peas...)
- 1 Onion, chopped
- 1 can diced Tomatoes
- 2 ¾ cup Vegetable Broth
- 12 ounces Green Beans

Directions:

1. Grease your IP with some cooking spray and add the onion.
2. Cook on SAUTE for a few minutes.
3. Stir in the remaining ingredients.
4. Close the lid and set the IP to MANUAL.
5. Cook the soup on HIGH for 5 minutes.
6. Release the pressure for 5 minutes.
7. Serve immediately.
8. Enjoy!

(Calories 100 | Total Fats 3g | Carbs 14g | Protein 5g | Fiber: 2g)

Squash and Potato Soup

(Total Time: 40 MIN | Serves: 4)

Ingredients:

- 2 cups cubed Sweet Potatoes
- 2 cups cubed Butternut Squash
- 1 Onion, diced
- 3 cups Vegetable Broth
- 2 tbsp Coconut Oil

Directions:

1. Melt the coconut oil in the IP on SAUTE.
2. Add the onions and cook for 3 minutes.
3. Add the potatoes and squash and cook for another minute.
4. Pour the broth over and close the lid.
5. Set the IP to MANUAL and cook on HIGH for 10 minutes.
6. Release the pressure naturally, about 10 minutes.
7. Blend the soup with a hand blender until smooth.
8. Serve immediately and enjoy!

(Calories 240 | Total Fats 9g | Carbs 35g | Protein 6.5g | Fiber: 3g)

Plantain and Red Bean Stew

(Total Time: 80 MIN | Serves: 4)

Ingredients:

- 2 Plantains, chopped
- ½ pound Dry Red Beans
- 1 Tomato, chopped
- 1 Onion, chopped

Directions:

1. Grease your Instant Pot with come cooking spray and saute the onions for a few minutes.
2. Stir in the beans.
3. Pour enough water to cover everything well.
4. Close the lid and set the IP to MANUAL.
5. Cook on HIGH for 30 minutes.
6. Let the pressure drop for 10 minutes.
7. Stir in the tomato and plantains.
8. Close the lid again and cook for another 30 minutes.
9. Again, release the pressure for 10 minutes.
10. Serve and enjoy!

(Calories 200 | Total Fats 4g | Carbs 15g | Protein 4g | Fiber: 3g)

Lentil Chili

(Total Time: 35 MIN | Serves: 6)

Ingredients:

- 1 Onion, diced
- 2 2/3 cups Lentils
- 28 ounces canned diced Tomatoes, undrained
- 1 tbsp Olive Oil
- 7 cups Vegetable Broth

Directions:

1. Heat the oil in your IP on SAUTE.
2. Add the onions and cook until they become soft, about 5 minutes.
3. Add tomatoes and cook for 1 more minute.
4. Stir in the remaining ingredients and close the lid.
5. Set the IP to MANUAL.
6. Cook on HIGH for 18 minutes.
7. Do a natural pressure release, about 10 minutes.
8. Serve and enjoy!

(Calories 320 | Total Fats 3g | Carbs 54g | Protein 18g | Fiber: 7g)

Orange, Sweet Potato & Chickpea Stew

(Total Time: 20 MIN | Serves: 6)

Ingredients:

- 1 pound diced Sweet Potatoes
- 30 ounces canned Chickpeas
- 4 cups Vegetable Broth
- 8 ounces Orange Juice
- 2 Onions, sliced

Directions:

1. Grease the Instant Pot with some cooking spray and cook the onions on SAUTE, until soft. You can also omit the cooking pray and soften the onions with some of the orange juice.
2. Stir in the remaining ingredients.
3. Close the lid and set the IP to MANUAL.
4. Cook the stew on HIGH for 5 minutes.
5. Release the pressure naturally, for about 10 minutes.
6. Serve and enjoy!

(Calories 240 | Total Fats 8g | Carbs 30g | Protein 8g | Fiber: 5g)

Pomodoro Soup

(Total Time: 25 MIN | Serves: 8)

Ingredients:

- 3 pounds Tomatoes, peeled and quartered
- 1 cup Coconut Cream
- 29 ounces Vegetable Broth
- 1 Onion, diced
- 3 tbsp Vegan Butter

Directions:

1. Melt the butter in the Instant Pot on SAUTE.
2. Add the onions and cook for 3-5 minutes.
3. Add the tomatoes and cook for 2 more minutes.
4. Close the lid and set the IP to SOUP.
5. Cook for 6 minutes.
6. Press CANCEL and wait a few minutes before doing a quick pressure release.
7. Stir in the coconut cream and set the IP to SAUTE.
8. Cook for 1 minute.
9. Blend the soup with a hand blender.
10. Serve and enjoy!

(Calories 300 | Total Fats 18g | Carbs 9.5g | Protein 11g | Fiber: 3g)

Corn and Onion Chowder

(Total Time: 45 MIN | Serves: 4)

Ingredients:

- 1 cup Coconut Milk
- 3 ½ cups Corn
- 2 Onions, diced
- 4 cups Vegetable Broth
- 2 tbsp Coconut Oil

Directions:

1. Melt the coconut oil in your Instant Pot on SAUTE.
2. Add the onions and cook for 5 minutes.
3. Add corn and broth, and give it a good stir to combine.
4. Close the lid and set the IP to MANUAL.
5. Cook for 5 minutes on HIGH.
6. Do a natural pressure release.
7. Stir in the coconut milk.
8. Close the lid and let the mixture sit for 5 minutes before serving.
9. Enjoy!

(Calories 197 | Total Fats 8g | Carbs 28g | Protein 5g | Fiber: 4g)

Leek, Broccoli, and Potato Soup

(Total Time: 20 MIN | Serves: 4)

Ingredients:

- 3 cups Broccoli Florets
- 1 cup sliced Leek
- 3 cups diced Potatoes
- 4 cups Vegetable Broth
- 2 tbsp Coconut Oil

Directions:

1. Melt the coconut oil in your Instant Pot on SAUTE.
2. Add the leeks and cook for 3 minutes.
3. Add broccoli, and potatoes, and pour the broth over.
4. Close the lid and set your IP to MANUAL.
5. Cook for 5 minutes on HIGH.
6. Release the pressure for 5 minutes.
7. Blend the soup with a hand blender until creamy and smooth.
8. Serve and enjoy!

(Calories 340 | Total Fats 7g | Carbs 20g | Protein 7g | Fiber: 3g)

Vegetable Recipes

Instant Ratatouille

(Total Time: 20 MIN | Serves: 4)

Ingredients:

- 2 medium Zucchini, sliced
- 2 small to medium Eggplants, sliced
- 3 Tomatoes, sliced
- 1 tbsp Olive Oil

Directions:

1. Pour some water into the Instant Pot, about 1-2 cups.
2. In a baking dish, arrange a layer of the zucchini.
3. Top with a layer of the tomatoes.
4. Place a layer of eggplant slices on top.
5. Continue laryering until you use all of the ingreidents.
6. Drizzle with olive oil.
7. Place the baking dish on the trivet and lower it.
8. Close the lid of the IP and set it to MANUAL.
9. Cook on HIGH for 10 minutes.
10. Serve and enjoy!

(Calories 180 | Total Fats 10g | Carbs 9.5g | Protein 2.5 g | Fiber: 2.4g)

Kale and Sweet Potatoes with Tofu

(Total Time: 45 MIN | Serves: 4)

Ingredients:

- 1 Sweet Potato, cubed
- 2 cups chopped Kale
- 8 ounces Tofu, cubed
- 2/3 cup Vegetable Broth
- 1 tbsp Tamari Sauce

Directions:

1. Add the tofu in your Instant Pot.
2. Drizzle with half of the tamari and some of the broth.
3. Cook for about 3 minutes on SAUTE.
4. Add the remaining ingredients and close the lid.
5. Set the IP to MANUAL.
6. Cook on HIGH for about 3 minutes.
7. Do a natural pressure release.
8. Serve and enjoy!

(Calories 130 | Total Fats 2.5g | Carbs 13g | Protein 11g | Fiber: 2g)

Pureed Chili Carrots

(Total Time: 25 MIN | Serves: 4)

Ingredients:

- 1 ½ pounds Carrots, chopped
- 1 tbsp Maple Syrup
- 1 tsp Chili Powder
- 1 ½ cups Water
- 1 tbsp Coconut Oil

Directions:

1. Pour the water into the Instant Pot.
2. Place the chopped carrots inside the steamer basket.
3. Lower the basket and close the lid.
4. Set the IP to MANUAL and cook for 4 minutes on HIGH.
5. Do a quick pressure release.
6. Transfer the carrots along with the remaining ingredients to a food processor.
7. Process until pureed and smooth.
8. Serve and enjoy!

(Calories 45 | Total Fats 1g | Carbs 11g | Protein 1g | Fiber: 1g)

Sesame Bok Choy

(Total Time: 5 MIN | Serves: 4)

Ingredients:

- 1 medium Bok Choy
- ½ tsp Sesame Oil
- 1 tsp Soy Sauce
- 2 tsp Sesame Seeds
- 1 ½ cups Water

Directions:

1. Pour the water into your IP.
2. Place the bok choy inside the steamer basket.
3. Lower the basket and close the lid.
4. Cook on HIGH for 4 minutes.
5. Do a quick pressure release.
6. Transfer the bok choy to a serving bowl.
7. Add the remaining ingredients and toss to coat well.
8. Serve and enjoy!

(Calories 54 | Total Fats 2g | Carbs 5g | Protein 3g | Fiber: 0.5g)

Lemon Artichokes

(Total Time: 40 MIN | Serves: 4)

Ingredients:

- 2 Artichokes
- 2 tbsp Dijon Mustard
- Juice of 1 Lemon
- 1 Lemon Wedge
- 1 ½ cups Water

Directions:

1. Pour the water into the Instant Pot.
2. Wash the artichokes and trim them.
3. Rub them with the lemon wedge and place inside the steamer basket.
4. Lower the basket and close the lid.
5. Set the IP to MANUAL.
6. Cook the artichokes on HIGH for 20 minutes.
7. Release the pressure naturally, for about 10 minutes.
8. Drizzle with the lemon juice.
9. Serve and enjoy!

(Calories 77 | Total Fats 0.2g | Carbs 17g | Protein 5.3g | Fiber: 3g)

Broccoli and Mushrooms

(Total Time: 15 MIN | Serves: 4)

Ingredients:

- 1 cup sliced Mushrooms
- 2 cups Broccoli Florets
- 2 tbsp Coconut Oil
- 1 cup Vegetable Broth
- 1 tbsp Soy Sauce

Directions:

1. Melt the coconut oil in your IP on SAUTE.
2. Add mushrooms and cook for 4-5 minutes.
3. Add broccoli and soy sauce and cook for 1 more minute.
4. Pour the broth over and close the lid.
5. Set the IP to MANUAL and cook on HIGH for 2 minutes.
6. Do a quick pressure release.
7. Serve the veggies drizzled with the cooking liquid.
8. Serve and enjoy!

(Calories 80.7 | Total Fats 7g | Carbs 3.9g | Protein 2.1g | Fiber: 1.6g)

Tomato and Tofu Bake

(Total Time: 10 MIN | Serves: 4)

Ingredients:

- 1 block of Tofu, crumbled
- 1 tbsp Italian Seasoning
- 1 can diced Tomatoes, undrained
- ½ cup Vegetable Broth
- 2 tbsp jarred Banana Pepper Rings

Directions:

1. Place all of the ingredients in the IP.
2. Give the mixture a good stir to incorporate everything well.
3. Close the lid and set your IP to MANUAL.
4. Cook for 4 minutes on HIGH.
5. Do a quick pressure release.
6. Serve and enjoy!

(Calories 140 | Total Fats 6g | Carbs 9g | Protein 11g | Fiber: 1g)

Potato Mash

(Total Time: 15 MIN | Serves: 4)

Ingredients:

- 4 Medium Potatoes
- ¼ cup Coconut Milk
- 2 tbsp Coconut Oil
- Pinch of Nutmeg

Directions:

1. Peel the potatoes and place them in the IP.
2. Add enough water to cover them.
3. Close the lid and set the IP to MANUAL.
4. Cook on HIGH for 8 minutes.
5. Do a quick pressure release.
6. Drain and mash the potatoes with a potato masher.
7. Stir in the remaining ingredients.
8. Serve and enjoy!

(Calories 210 | Total Fats 7.2g | Carbs 34g | Protein 3.7g | Fiber: 5g)

Main Dish Recipes

Vegan White Pizza

(Total Time: 15 MIN | Serves: 2)

Ingredients:

- 1 store-bought Pizza Crust
- ¼ cup Vegan Alfredo Sauce
- 1 tsp chopped Oregano
- ½ cup shredded Vegan Cheese
- 1 ½ cups Water

Directions:

1. Pour the water into your IP. Lower the trivet.
2. Line a baking dish that can fit into the IP with parchment paper.
3. Roll out the pizza crust and place inside the baking dish.
4. Spread the Alfredo sauce over the crust and sprinkle the cheese over.
5. Top with chopped oregano.
6. Place the dish on the lowered trivet and close the lid of the IP.
7. Set the IP to MANUAL and cook the pizza for 5 minutes on HIGH.

8. Do a quick pressure release.
9. Serve and enjoy!

(Calories 390 | Total Fats 20g | Carbs 30g | Protein 8g |Fiber: 2g)

Mini Vegan Shephard's Pie

(Total Time: 20 MIN | Serves: 4)

Ingredients:

- 1 cup diced Onion
- 2 cups steamed and mashed Cauliflower
- 1 cup grated Potatoes
- 1 cup diced Tomatoes
- 1 ½ cup Water

Directions:

1. Add a splash of water to your IP and set it to SAUTE.
2. Add the onions and cook for 2 minutes.
3. Add the potatoes and cook on SAUTE for 5 minutes, stirring frequently.
4. Stir in the tomatoes and cook for 3 more minutes.
5. Divide the mixture between 4 greased ramekins.
6. Top with the mashed potatoes.
7. Pour the water into the IP and lower the trivet.
8. Place the ramekins on the trivet and close the lid.
9. Cook on HIGH for 5 minutes.
10. Serve and enjoy!

(Calories 225 | Total Fats 14g | Carbs 5g | Protein 12g | Fiber: 0.3g)

Mushroom Pasta

(Total Time: 20 MIN | Serves: 4)

Ingredients:

- 1 ½ cups sliced Mushrooms
- 1 cup Coconut Milk
- 2 cups Water
- 1 tsp Arrowroot
- 2 cups Pasta, uncooked

Directions:

1. Add a splash of the coconut milk in the IP and set it to SAUTE.
2. Add mushrooms and cook for a few minutes.
3. Stir in the rest of the milk, water, and pasta.
4. Close the lid and set the IP to MANUAL.
5. Cook on HIGH for 7 minutes.
6. Do a quick pressure release and set the IP to SAUTE.
7. Whisk in the arrowroot and cook until the sauce thickens a bit.
8. Serve and enjoy!

(Calories 452 | Total Fats 15g | Carbs 34g | Protein 15g | Fiber: 3g)

Basil Risotto

(Total Time: 30 MIN | Serves: 6)

Ingredients:

- 1 ½ tbsp Olive Oil
- 1 Onion, chopped
- 28 ounces Vegetable Broth
- 12 ounces Arborio Rice
- 1 ½ cups chopped Basil

Directions:

1. Heat the oil in the IP on SAUTE.
2. Add the onions and cook for 3 minutes.
3. Add the rice and cook for another minute.
4. Pour the broth over, give it a stir, and close the lid.
5. Cook on RICE for 15 minutes.
6. Do a quick pressure release.
7. Stir in the basil and cook on SAUTE for another minute.
8. Serve and enjoy!

(Calories 260 | Total Fats 5g | Carbs 46g | Protein 7.8g | Fiber: 2g)

Vegan Cheese and Asparagus Pasta

(Total Time: 20 MIN | Serves: 4)

Ingredients:

- 1 cup shredded Vegan Cheese
- 2 cups Pasta
- 6 Asparagus Spears, chopped
- ½ cup Vegan Alfredo Sauce
- 3 ½ cups Veggie Broth

Directions:

1. Combine the pasta, asparagus, and broth, in the IP.
2. Close the lid and set it to MANUAL.
3. Cook on HIGH for 7 minutes.
4. Release the pressure quickly.
5. Drain the pasta and return it to the IP.
6. Stir in the sauce and cheese.
7. Cook on SAUTE for 2 minutes.
8. Serve and enjoy!

(Calories 480 | Total Fats 12g | Carbs 39g | Protein 8g | Fiber: 2g)

Carrot and Sweet Potato Medley

(Total Time: 20 MIN | Serves: 4)

Ingredients:

- 2 tbsp Olive Oil
- 2 pounds Sweet Potatoes, cubed
- 1 Onion, chopped
- 2 pounds Baby Carrots, halved
- 1 cup Veggie Broth

Directions:

1. Heat the oil in your IP on SAUTE.
2. Add the onion and cook until soft, about 5 minutes.
3. Add the remaining ingredients, stir to combine, and close the lid.
4. Set the IP to MANUAL and cook on HIGH for 8 minutes.
5. Release the pressure quickly.
6. Serve and enjoy!

(Calories 413 | Total Fats 7.5g | Carbs 76g | Protein 7g | Fiber: 13g)

Pesto Farfale

(Total Time: 10 MIN | Serves: 4)

Ingredients:

- 12 ounces Farfale
- ¾ cup Vegan Pesto
- 4 cups Water
- 1 cup Cherry Tomatoes

Directions:

1. Combine the farfalle and water in your IP.
2. Close the lid and set the pot to MANUAL.
3. Cook on HIGH for 7 minutes.
4. Do a quick pressure release.
5. Drain the pasta and return to the pot.
6. Stir in the pesto sauce and cook on SAUTE for 1 more minute.
7. Quarter the cherry tomatoes and stir into the pasta.
8. Serve and enjoy!

(Calories 390 | Total Fats 9g | Carbs 40g | Protein 8g | Fiber: 1g)

Mexican Rice Casserole

(Total Time: 35 MIN | Serves: 4)

Ingredients:

- 1 cup Black Beans, soaked overnight and drained
- 5 cups Water
- 2 cups Brown Rice
- 6 ounces Salsa Paste
- 2 tsp Cumin

Directions:

1. Combine all of the ingredients in your Instant Pot.
2. Close the lid and set the IP to MANUAL.
3. Cook on HIGH for 28 minutes.
4. Do a quick pressure release.
5. Serve garnished with lime and cilantro, if desired.
6. Enjoy!

(Calories 322 | Total Fats 2g | Carbs 60 g | Protein 6g | Fiber: 8g)

Burger and Patties

Cauliflower Patties

(Total Time: 25 MIN | Serves: 4)

Ingredients:

- 1 cup shredded Vegan Cheese
- 1 Cauliflower Head, chopped
- 1 cup ground Almonds
- 3 tbsp Olive Oil
- 1 ½ cups Water

Directions:

1. Pour the water into the IP.
2. Place the cauliflower in the steamer basket and lower it.
3. Close the lid and cook on HIGH for 5 minutes.
4. Do a quick pressure release.
5. Drain it well and ground in a food processor
6. Stir in the cheese and almonds.
7. Shape patties out of the mixture.
8. Heat half of the olive oil in the IP on SAUTE and add half of the patties.
9. Cook until golden on all sides.
10. Repeat with the other batch.

11. Serve and enjoy!

(Calories 120 | Total Fats 7g | Carbs 4.7g | Protein 2.8g | Fiber: 2g)

Mixed Veggie Patties

(Total Time: 25 MIN | Serves: 4)

Ingredients:

- 1 mixed Veggie Frozen Bag
- 1 cup Cauliflower Florets
- 2 tbsp Olive Oil
- 1 ½ cups Water
- 1 cup Flax Meal

Directions:

1. Pour the water into the IP.
2. Place the mixed veggies and cauliflower in the steamer basket.
3. Close the lid and cook on HIGH for 4-5 minutes.
4. Do a quick pressure release.
5. Drain and mash with a potato masher.
6. Stir in the flax meal.
7. Shape 4 patties out of the mixture.
8. Wipe the IP clean and hat the oil in it on SAUTE.
9. Add the patties and cook for about 3 minute per side, until golden.
10. Serve and enjoy!

(Calories 220| Total Fats 10g | Carbs 6g | Protein 4g | Fiber: 3g)

Potato and Scallion Patties

(Total Time: 30 MIN | Serves: 6)

Ingredients:

- 9 ounces Potatoes, boiled and mashed
- 1 tbsp Coconut Cream
- 4 ounces Scallions, chopped
- 1 Olive Oil
- 1/3 cup Flour

Directions:

1. Mix together the potatoes, coconut cream, scallions, and flour.
2. Make patties out of the mixture.
3. Heat the olive oil in the IP on SAUTE.
4. Add the patties and cook for about 3 minutes per side.
5. Serve and enjoy!

(Calories 130 | Total Fats 5.5g | Carbs 15g | Protein 5g | Fiber: 2g)

Eggplant Burgers

(Total Time: 25 MIN | Serves: 4)

Ingredients:

- 1 Large Eggplant
- ½ cup Panko Breadcrumbs
- 2 tbsp Mustard
- 2 tbsp Olive Oil
- 1 cup Water

Directions:

1. Pour the water into the IP.
2. Trim and wash the eggplants, then slice them into 4 rounds.
3. Place the eggplants in the water and close the lid.
4. Cook on HIGH for 2 minutes.
5. Do a quick pressure release.
6. Discard the cooking liquid and drain the eggplant rounds.
7. Brush them with mustard and coat with panko.
8. Heat the oil in the IP and add the eggplant burgers.
9. Cook until golden on all sides.
10. Serve in buns or on their own.
11. Enjoy!

(Calories 170| Total Fats 36g | Carbs 26g | Protein 15g |Fiber: 6g)

Beet and Chickpea Burger Patties

(Total Time: 15 MIN | Serves: 4)

Ingredients:

- 1 Beetroot, shredded
- 1 cup canned Chickpeas, drained
- 1 cup Almond Flour
- 1 tbsp Olive Oil
- 3 tbsp Vegan Mayo

Directions:

1. Combine the chickpeas and beetroot in your food processor.
2. Pulse for a minute.
3. Stir in the almond flour and vegan mayo.
4. Make 4 patties out of the mixture.
5. Heat the oil in the IP on SAUTE.
6. Add the patties and cook for 3 minutes per side.
7. Serve and enjoy!

(Calories 570| Total Fats 48g | Carbs 25g | Protein 9g | Fiber: 6g)

Zucchini Burgers

(Total Time: 25 MIN | Serves: 4)

Ingredients:

- 1 Large Zucchini, shredded
- ¼ cup Flour
- ½ cup mashed Potatoes
- 2 tbsp Olive Oil
- ¼ cup Panko Breadcrumbs

Directions:

1. Heat the oil in the Instant Pot on SAUTE.
2. Meanwhile, combine the remaining ingredients.
3. Make 4 patties out of the mixture.
4. Cook on SAUTE for 3 minutes.
5. Flip over and cook for another 2-3 minutes.
6. If you want to, you can add a few tablespoons of water, close the lid, bring to a pressure for a minute, and then release it quickly. This will make the patties softer.
7. Serve and enjoy!

(Calories 300 | Total Fats 5g | Carbs 14g | Protein 3g | Fiber: 2g)

Red Bean Burger Patties

(Total Time: 25 MIN | Serves: 2)

Ingredients:

- 1 cup Red Beans
- 2 cups Water
- 1 ½ tbsp Olive Oil
- 1 cup mashed Potatoes
- ¼ cup Panko Breadcrumbs

Directions:

1. Pour the water into the IP.
2. Add the beans and close the lid.
3. Cook on HIGH for 15 minutes.
4. Do a quick pressure release.
5. Drain and place in a food processor.
6. Add the breadcrumbs and potatoes and pulse until well combined.
7. Form 2 patties out of the mixture.
8. Heat the oil in the IP on SAUTE.
9. Cook the patties until golden.
10. Serve and enjoy!

(Calories 250| Total Fats 2g| Carbs 48g | Protein 10.8g | Fiber: 10.8g)

Corn Patties

(Total Time: 25 MIN | Serves: 4)

Ingredients:

- 1 cup canned Corn, drained
- 1 Carrot, chopped
- 3 Potatoes, cubed
- ½ cup Panko Breadcrumbs

Directions:

1. Place the carrots and potatoes in the IP and add enough water to cover them.
2. Close the lid and cook on HIGH for 5 minutes.
3. Do a quick pressure release and transfer them to a food processor.
4. Add the corn and breadcrumbs and process until well incorporated.
5. Make 4 patties out of the mixture.
6. Wipe the IP clean and grease with some cooking spray.
7. Add the patties and cook until super golden, about 4 minutes per side.
8. Serve and enjoy!

(Calories 202| Total Fats 1.3g | Carbs 44g | Protein 5.9g | Fiber: 5.4g)

Sauce Recipes

Chili Sauce

(Total Time: 25 MIN | Serves: 6)

Ingredients:

- ½ cup Apple Cider Vinegar
- ½ tsp Salt
- 6 ounces Hot Peppers

Directions:

1. Remove the stems from the peppers and chop them.
2. Place them in your Instant Pot and add a splash of vinegar.
3. Cook on SAUTE for 3 minutes.
4. Add the remaining ingredients and close the lid.
5. Set the IP to MANUAL and cook on HIGH for 15 minutes.
6. Do a quick pressure release.
7. Blend the sauce with a hand blender.
8. Serve and enjoy!

(Calories 2| Total Fats 0g | Carbs 0.7g | Protein 1g |Fiber: 0g)

White Sauce

(Total Time: 20 MIN | Serves: 4)

Ingredients:

- 12 ounces Cauliflower Florets
- 2 tbsp Almond Milk
- ¼ tsp Garlic Salt
- ½ cup Water
- ¼ tsp Pepper

Directions:

1. Combine everything but the milk in your Instant Pot.
2. Close the lid and set your IP to MANUAL.
3. Cook on HIGH for 3 minutes.
4. Blend the sauce with a hand blender.
5. Stir in the almond milk.
6. Serve and enjoy!

(Calories 40| Total Fats 0g | Carbs 3g | Protein 3g | Fiber: 1g)

Lentil Marinara Sauce

(Total Time: 25 MIN | Serves: 8)

Ingredients:

- 1/3 cup Lentils
- 1 Sweet Potato, diced
- 14 ounces crushed Tomatoes
- 1 cup Water
- ½ tsp Garlic Salt

Directions:

1. Set your IP to SAUTE.
2. Add tomatoes, garlic, potato, and lentils, and saute for 3 minutes.
3. Pour the water over, stir to combine, and close the lid.
4. Cook on HIGH for 13 minutes.
5. Release the pressure naturally.
6. Blend the mixture with a hand blender.
7. Serve and enjoy!

(Calories 85 | Total Fats 0g | Carbs 7g | Protein 2.5 Fiber: 1.5g)

Applesauce

(Total Time: 30 MIN | Serves: 4)

Ingredients:

- 12 Apples, cored and quartered
- 1 tbsp Maple Syrup
- Juice from ½ Lemon
- 1 cup Water
- 2 tbsp Ghee

Directions:

1. Place all of the ingredients in your Instant Pot.
2. Stir to combine, close the lid and set the IP to MANUAL.
3. Cook the mixture on HIGH for 3 minutes.
4. Do a natural pressure release.
5. Discard half of the cooking liquid.
6. Blend with a hand blender but make sure to leave some chunks.
7. Serve and enjoy!

(Calories 70 | Total Fats 1.5g | Carbs 19g | Protein 0.5g | Fiber: 4g)

Bean Bolognese Sauce

(Total Time: 15 MIN | Serves: 4)

Ingredients:

- 1 pound canned Beans
- ¼ cup chopped Parsley
- 1 can Pasta Sauce
- 3 Basil Leaves, chopped
- 3 Garlic Cloves, minced

Directions:

1. Combine all of the ingredients in your Instant Pot.
2. Choose the MANUAL cooking mode.
3. Close the lid and cook on HIGH for 8 minutes.
4. Do a quick pressure release.
5. Serve and enjoy!

(Calories 360 | Total Fats 10g | Carbs 30g | Protein 7g | Fiber: 5g)

Tomato and Basil Sauce

(Total Time: 40 MIN | Serves: 4)

Ingredients:

- ½ cup chopped Basil
- 3 Garlic Cloves, minced
- 2 ½ pounds Roma Tomatoes, diced
- ¼ cup Vegetable Broth
- 1 tbsp Olive Oil

Directions:

1. Heat the olive oil in your IP n SAUTE.
2. Add the garlic and cook for 1 minute.
3. Add the remaining ingredients and stir well to combine.
4. Close the lid and set the Instant Pot to MANUAL.
5. Cook on HIGH for 10 minutes.
6. Do a quick pressure release.
7. Set the IP to SAUTE again.
8. Cook for 5 more minutes.
9. Blend with a hand blender, if desired.
10. Serve and enjoy!

(Calories 40| Total Fats 1.5g | Carbs 5g | Protein 1.7g |Fiber: 1g)

Mixed Veggie Sauce

(Total Time: 25 MIN | Serves: 4)

Ingredients:

- 4 Tomatoes, chopped
- 2 Bell Peppers, chopped
- 2 Carrots, chopped
- 1 Leek, sliced
- 1 cup Veggie Broth

Directions:

1. Add a splash of broth to the IP and set it to SAUTE.
2. Add leek and bell peppers and cook for 3 minutes.
3. Add the tomatoes and carrots and cook for another 3 minutes.
4. Pour the broth over and give it a stir.
5. Closet he lid and set it to MANUAL.
6. Cook on HIGH for 6 minutes.
7. Release the pressure naturally.
8. Discard half of the cooking liquid before blending the sauce with a hand blender.
9. Serve and enjoy!

(Calories 120 | Total Fats 4g | Carbs 4g | Protein 3g | Fiber: 1g)

Vanilla Caramel Sauce

(Total Time: 20 MIN | Serves: 4)

Ingredients:

- 3 tbsp Coconut Oil
- 1 tsp Vanilla Extract
- 1 cup Sugar
- 1/3 cup Condensed Coconut Milk
- 1/3 cup Water

Directions:

1. Combine the water and sugar in your Instant Pot.
2. Set it to SAUTE and cook for 13 minutes.
3. Stir in the vanilla, coconut oil, and milk.
4. Whisk until it is real smooth.
5. Immediately transfer to a heatproof glass container.
6. Let cool completely before serving.
7. Enjoy!

(Calories 80 | Total Fats 1.5g | Carbs 15g | Protein 0g | Fiber: 1g)

Snack and Appetizers Recipes

Lime and Garlic Kale "Chips"

(Total Time: 15 MIN| Serves: 6)

Ingredients:

- 1 pound Kale
- 3 Garlic Cloves, minced
- 2 tbsp Lime Juice
- ½ cup Water
- 1 tbsp Olive Oil

Directions:

1. Heat the oil in your IP on SAUTE.
2. Add garlic and cook until fragrant.
3. Place the kale in a baking dish and drizzle the garlic over.
4. Pour the water into the IP and lower the trivet.
5. Place the baking dish on the trivet and close the lid.
6. Cook on HIGH for 5 minutes.
7. Discard the water, wipe the IP clean and transfer the kale to the IP.
8. Cook on SAUTE for 5 more minutes.
9. Drizzle with lime juice and serve.
10. Enjoy!

(Calories 66| Total Fats 4g | Carbs 7.5g | Protein 2.3g | Fiber: 2.4g)

Street Corn on the Cob

(Total Time: 10 MIN | Serves: 4)

Ingredients:

- 4 Sweet Corn on the Cob
- Juice of 2 Limes
- 6 tbsp Coconut Cream
- 1 tsp Chili Powder
- 2 cups Water

Directions:

1. Pour the water into the IP.
2. Place the corn inside the steamer basket.
3. Lower the basket and close the lid.
4. Cook for 3 minutes on HIGH.
5. Do a quick pressure release.
6. Whisk the remaining ingredients.
7. Drizzle the corn with the mixture.
8. Serve and enjoy!

(Calories 130| Total Fats 5g | Carbs 16g | Protein 9g |Fiber: 2.5g)

Turmeric Sweet Potato Sticks

(Total Time: 20 MIN | Serves: 1)

Ingredients:

- 1 Sweet Potato
- 1 tsp Turmeric Powder
- 1 tbsp Coconut Oil
- 1 ½ cups Water

Directions:

1. Pour the water into the IP.
2. Peel the potato and cut it into strips.
3. Place in the steamer basket and lower it.
4. Close the lid and set the IP to MANUAL.
5. Cook on HIGH for 5 minutes.
6. Do a quick pressure release.
7. Discard the water and wipe the IP clean.
8. Melt the coconut oil in it on SAUTE and add the potatoes.
9. Sprinkle with turmeric and cook for about 5 more minutes, turning once.
10. Serve and enjoy!

(Calories 136 | Total Fats 0.2g | Carbs 16g | Protein 1g | Fiber: 2g)

Boiled Peanuts

(Total Time: 80 MIN | Serves: 8)

Ingredients:

- 1 pound Raw Peanuts
- ¼ cup Sea Salt

Directions:

1. Clean the peanuts and remove their roots and twigs.
2. Place them in your Instant Pot and sprinkle the salt over.
3. Add enough water to cover completely.
4. Close the lid and set the IP to MANUAL.
5. Cook on HIGH for 70 minutes.
6. Release the pressure for 5 minutes.
7. Serve and enjoy!

(Calories 100| Total Fats 10g | Carbs 8g | Protein 7g |Fiber: 3g)

Mini Mac and Cheese

(Total Time: 17 MIN | Serves: 4)

Ingredients:

- 8 ounces Whole-Wheat Macaroni
- ¾ cups shredded Vegan Cheese
- 2 cups Water

Directions:

1. Pour the water into the IP and place the macaroni inside.
2. Close the lid and set the Instant Pot to RICE.
3. Cook for 5 minutes.
4. Do a quick pressure release.
5. Add the cheese and set the IP to SAUTE.
6. Cook for 2 more minutes.
7. Divide between 4 small bowls.
8. Serve and enjoy!

(Calories 132 | Total Fats 5.5g | Carbs 15g | Protein 7g | Fiber: 1.5g)

Turnip Alfredo Dip

(Total Time: 10 MIN | Serves: 4)

Ingredients:

- 2 Large Turnips, cubed
- 1 cup Vegan Alfredo Sauce
- ¼ cup chopped Chives
- 1 cup Water
- ½ tsp Garlic Salt

Directions:

1. Pour the water into the IP.
2. Add the turnip cubes and close the lid.
3. Cook on HIGH for 5 minutes.
4. Do a quick pressure release.
5. Mash with a potato masher.
6. Stir in the alfredo sauce, chives, and garlic salt.
7. Serve with crackers or veggies.
8. Enjoy!

(Calories 110 | Total Fats 8g | Carbs 11g | Protein 4g | Fiber: 2g)

Instant Potato Slices

(Total Time: 15 MIN | Serves: 4)

Ingredients:

- 2 Large Potatoes
- Salt, as needed
- 2 tbsp Coconut Oil
- Water, as needed

Directions:

1. Wash the potatoes well and slice them thinly.
2. Place in the steamer basket.
3. Pour the water into the IP and lower the basket.
4. Close the lid and cook on HIGH for 2 minutes.
5. Do a quick pressure release.
6. Discard the water and wipe the IP clean.
7. Set it to SAUTE and melt the coconut oil in it.
8. Add the potato slices and sprinkle with some salt.
9. Cook for a few minutes per side. If you want them to be crispier, place them under a broiler for a minute or two.
10. Serve and enjoy!

(Calories 185 | Total Fats 7g | Carbs 29g | Protein 3.1g | Fiber: 4.4g)

Candied Pecans

(Total Time: 30 MIN | Serves: 4)

Ingredients:

- 2 cups Pecan Halves
- ½ cup plus 1 tbsp Water
- 3 tbsp Maple Syrup
- ½ tsp Cinnamon

Directions:

1. Combine the pecans, maple syrup, cinnamon, and 1 tbsp water, in the IP.
2. Set it to SAUTE and cook the pecans for 5 minutes.
3. Line a baking dish and transfer the pecans to it.
4. Pour the water into the IP and lower the trivet.
5. Place the dish on the trivet.
6. Close the lid and cook on HIGH for 12 minutes.
7. Serve and enjoy!

(Calories 250 | Total Fats 38g | Carbs 8g | Protein 5g | Fiber: 3g)

Dessert Recipes

Almond and Chocolate Candy

(Total Time: 30 MIN | Serves: 6)

Ingredients:

- 14 ounces Condensed Coconut Milk
- 12 ounces Dark Chocolate Chips
- 2 cups Water
- 1 cup chopped Almonds

Directions:

1. Pour the water into the IP.
2. Combine the chocolate chips and milk in a dish that is heatproof.
3. Cover the dish with foil and place in the IP.
4. Close the lid and cook on HIGH for 3 minutes.
5. Uncover and fold in the almonds.
6. Line a baking sheet with a piece of parchment paper.
7. With a teaspoon, drop the candy onto the paper.
8. Place in the freezer to set.
9. Serve and enjoy!

(Calories 122| Total Fats 6g | Carbs 16g | Protein 3g |Fiber: 2g)

Banana Bread

(Total Time: 55 MIN | Serves: 12)

Ingredients:

- 4 Bananas, mashed
- 2 cups Self-Rising Flour
- 1/3 cup chopped Walnuts, optional
- 3 tbsp melted Vegan Butter
- 3 tbsp Sugar

Directions:

1. Pour some water into the IP, about 1-2 cups.
2. Whisk together the remaining ingredients in a bowl.
3. Grease a loaf pan and pour the batter into it.
4. Place the loaf pan on the lowered trivet and close the lid.
5. Cook for 40 minutes on MANUAL.
6. Do a quick pressure release.
7. Serve and enjoy!

(Calories 105 | Total Fats 4g | Carbs 13g | Protein 2g | Fiber: 3g)

Stuffed Peaches

(Total Time: 35 MIN | Serves: 6)

Ingredients:

- 6 Peaches
- ¼ cup Cassava Flour
- ¼ cup Maple Syrup
- 2 tbsp Vegan Butter
- 1 ½ cups Water

Directions:

1. Pour the water into the IP.
2. Slice off the top of the peaches and discard the pits.
3. In a bowl, combine the flour, maple, and butter.
4. Divide this mixture between the peaches.
5. Place the peaches in the steamer basket.
6. Lower the basket and close the lid.
7. Cook on HIGH for 3 minutes.
8. Do a quick pressure release.
9. Serve and enjoy!

(Calories 143 | Total Fats 5g | Carbs 25g | Protein 1.5g | Fiber: 3g)

Cherry Pie

(Total Time: 45 MIN | Serves: 6)

Ingredients:

- 1 9-inch double Pie Crust (made with Vegan ingredients only)
- 2 cups Water
- 4 cups pitted Cherries
- 4 tbsp Quick Tapioca
- 1 cup Sugar

Directions:

1. Pour the water into the IP. Lower the trivet.
2. In a bowl, combine the cherries, sugar and tapioca.
3. Roll out one of the pie crusts and place at the bottom of a lined and greased pan.
4. Pour the cherry filling over.
5. Slice the other crust into strips and arrange them pie-style, over the cherries.
6. Place the dish on the trivet and close the lid.
7. Cook for 18 minutes on MANUAL.
8. Do a quick pressure release.
9. Serve and enjoy!

(Calories 390 | Total Fats 12g | Carbs 70g | Protein 2g | Fiber: 1.6g)

Blueberry Lemon Compote

(Total Time: 2 hours and 50 MIN | Serves: 4)

Ingredients:

- ¾ cup Coconut Sugar
- 2 tbsp Cornstarch
- 2 cups Frozen Blueberries
- Juice of ½ Lemon
- 2 tbsp Water

Directions:

1. Combine the blueberries, lemon and sugar, in your IP.
2. Close the lid and set the IP to MANUAL.
3. Cook on HIGH for 3 minutes.
4. DO a natural pressure release.
5. Whisk together the water and cornstarch and whisk into the compote.
6. Cook on SAUTE for a few minutes, until thickened.
7. Serve and enjoy!

(Calories 220 | Total Fats 0.3g | Carbs 61g | Protein 1.2g | Fiber: 4g)

Apple Tart

(Total Time: 45 MIN | Serves: 8)

Ingredients:

- 3 cups Sliced Apples
- ½ cup Sugar
- ½ cup plus 2 tbsp Vegan Butter
- 2 cups Flour
- 1 ½ cups Water

Directions:

1. Pour the water into the IP.
2. In a bowl, combine the flour, 6 tbsp of the butter, and half of the sugar.
3. Press the mixture into the bottom of a greased baking dish.
4. Place the dish on the trivet and close the lid.
5. Cook for 3 minutes on HIGH.
6. Do a quick pressure release.
7. Arrange the apple slices on top of the crust.
8. Melt the remaining butter and combine it with the sugar.
9. Drizzle over the apples.
10. Place in the IP and cook on HIGH for 25 minutes.
11. Do a quick pressure release.
12. Serve and enjoy!

(Calories 300 | Total Fats 25g | Carbs: 20g | Protein 7g | Fiber: 3g)

Simple Apple and Coconut Balls
(Total Time: 15 MIN | Serves: 6)

Ingredients:

- 2 Apples, grated
- 1 cup Coconut Flakes
- 2 tbsp Cocoa Powder
- ½ cup chopped Walnuts
- ¼ cup Maple Syrup

Directions:

1. Combine the apples and maple syrup in the IP.
2. Close the lid and cook on HIGH for 2 minutes.
3. Do a quick pressure release.
4. Let cool until safe to handle.
5. Stir in the remaining ingredients.
6. Make balls out of the mixture.
7. Coat the balls with extra coconut flakes, if desired.
8. Serve and enjoy!

(Calories 196| Total Fats 12g | Carbs: 23g | Protein 2.4g | Fiber: 3.3g)

Chocolate Muffins

(Total Time: 30 MIN | Serves: 6)

Ingredients:

- ¼ cup Sweetened Cocoa Powder
- 1 cup Flaxseed Meal
- ½ cup Pumpkin Puree
- 1 ½ cups Water
- ¼ cup melted Coconut Oil

Directions:

1. Pour the water into the IP.
2. Whisk the remaining ingredients in a bowl.
3. Divide the batter between 6 muffin cups.
4. Place the muffin cups on the rack and close the lid.
5. Set the Instant Pot to MANUAL.
6. Cook on HIGH for 18 minutes.
7. Do a quick pressure release.
8. Serve and enjoy!

(Calories 193| Total Fats 14g | Carbs: 8g | Protein 7g | Fiber: 3g)

Conclusion

Now that your recipe folder is richer by 80 delightful dishes that do not require more than 5 ingredients, you can prepare amazing delicacies without having to worry about stocking your kitchen first.

I hope that this book was able to help you see how easy you can cook with a few ingredients in the Instant Pot, even when you are vegan.

Did you find these recipes yummy? Leave a review and share your thoughts with the others. Your feedback is greatly appreciated.

Thank you and happy pressure cooking!

Printed in the USA
CPSIA information can be obtained
at www.ICGtesting.com
LVHW021123250124
769912LV00059B/1646